poems

Richmond *Alexander* Lattimore, 1906-

poems.

Ann Arbor

The University of Michigan Press

to Alice

Some of these poems have appeared, copyrighted, in various magazines, to all of whom I am indebted for permission to reprint, with occasional revisions. The poems in question have appeared as follows:

ACCENT: A Letter to Twelve People

GLASS HILL: Invictus

HARPER'S: New Homes

THE HUDSON REVIEW: Hercules at the Crossroads, The Bridge at Arta, Pandora, Demeter in the Fields, Legend for a Shield

THE KENYON REVIEW: Waiting for the Barbarians, Loutsa Beach

THE NATION: Epigraphical Note

THE NEW YORKER: North Philadelphia Trenton and New York, Good Speed for Southward Voyagers, Omsk, Ona, Hara-kiri, Rise and Shine, Anniversary, The Shadowgraphs

POETRY (Chicago): Marginals, Search, Sea Changes, Note on the L & N, Romantic Landscape with Story, The Brink, Leilah, Return of the Image, Two Octobers

THE QUARTERLY REVIEW OF LITERATURE: The Wounded

THE SATURDAY REVIEW: Tudor Portrait, Captive, Autumn Equinox, It

THE SOUTHERN REVIEW: Glaukos, In the Beginning

BEST POEMS OF 1955 (Borestone Mountain Awards, Stanford University Press): North Philadelphia Trenton and New York, Loutsa Beach

Contents

1

2

3

4

5

1

North Philadelphia Trenton and New York

Thin steel, in paired lines forever mated, cuts,
forks and crosses, catches blue light, threads a station and a yard,
finds a bridge across the winter Schuylkill lithograph,
slips by the winter boardings, the chimney pots, the dirty
windowpanes and chimneys cut aslant for factories
either way aside.

        Now square your panes, look
large to wheel the brittle gray, the deep
horizon up. The prison steps into your square, and runs beside,
and drops away. The nunnery, the monastery after it,
fleetly shine, dip, recover, and are gone,
as houses in precise astonished rows come out,
sit up and solidify, stare, and are politely wheeled away.
Under bridge and under wheel the Delaware floats down
ice cakes, watched by the gilt glitter of the Capitol.

North now, sky change on earth angle altering,
color of iron blooms on spinneys, Breughel snow and brown tree
authenticate the high parallel.

        In North Jersey, flat, endlessly
arranged in silver gas cylinders, shine of plane wing, deep
dirty and deliberate rivers grope between meadows
where the catkins keep good order and the posters march beside you,
and the turnpike loping near on legs of pylons stays to race you,
and the hill with houses slides to meet you.

        The tunnel: you are gone,
and the bright winter sky as from a tube of indigo is squeezed away.

/ 3 /

Good Speed for Southward Voyagers

Now as you lose our sands, banks, fogs, and north,
may all Atlantic graces bless your prow
and progress forth;
Boreas sleep and bergs recede, gulls follow,
and all that's debonair at sea rise on your bow;

grave sister steamers salute with formal dip
of colors; wake-wings foam and murmur and submerge
behind your ship,
where dimly you discern at the far verge
some dripping Cytherea of the calms emerge.

Ah yes, may strange and benign sea monsters keep
you, and helmed, armed, and bosomy wind-cherubs, four
at the four corners of the deep,
bulging where blue is blue forevermore,
wave you with tridents to the Mediterranean shore.

A Letter to Twelve People

Bring back the early summer when you come,
and nine o'clock, and the gray angles
of towers breaking gleams along wet cobbles,
and lamps spilling on tangles

of water plied like rope; and bring the night
kneeling quietly on Witham, and the strain
of ivy on the broken cloister, and bring
the drip of water, and the after-rain

stillness of thick trees sleeping in the stream
on their own quiet idols there; and you
will float these gifts along your path for me.
These are the things we knew:

a bridge, a weir, an inn, a fallen tree;
the wakening lights a net laid slack
on the gray city, and all that was held in these.
Bring them when you come back.

Mid-Continental

Here, stuck on a green and brown hillside,
confined only by soft clumps on skylines, mound
and fault; by high hawk-ridden air, the bright well whose
      purpling thunders bud and hide
the grown edge; by near walnuts green under dust; lapped in sound

of blond country summer; reaping noises, far dogs and cattle; rain
stepping hushed in distances; here in half-across, the self-spelled
and self-mirrored, the narcissus brain
labors to imagine beyond eyescape's small miles. Oh, we are held

and smeared like flies by water on the sticky wheel
of what we were and what we are. We dream
more than remember how, east and west, the tossed halves of the
      Ocean seal
the brown in blue; how dawn there crowds our noon, stars swim

before our sunset. But there still the sea moon pulls her black
      tides
and our big ball, set with water-queens heading the white-hilled
bulge, turns always; and always his grand downside
holds blue water close upon him, not pinned with rock or
      stanchion, no drop spilled.

Marginals

To me lying near sleep, at the pale edge
of dark, sounds wrestle the gray beyond, and trains
at the outer margin slide and weave, the diesels
shudder their strings of cars and eat their noisy
miles, and farmlights star the black between.

To me lying near sleep the near leaves bind
my walls in hush of green gloom merged in still
and ebony and humming waves of leafed
midnight, where the small insect noises drown
in those deep currents that close in my walls.

To me lying near sleep the shuttered blinds
spill in a float of morning colors, wash
and rinse my eyes, disturb the escape of dreams
upon the white awakeness lying beside
my wakening in blithe birdsong and drenched day.

Search

The way a diver ropes
his pattern in the cool green
shadows woven in water
the arms develop
blue curves and puzzled arcs;
and the water torn above
gives his eyes to the sun
and the kneeling bay
and the white rocks drenched at the base
and the gazing ships;
and the arms design
their dripping action again
stroke and overstroke
the legs in foam blurred
driving weight in water.
In the sun on the wet planks
eyes and body
remember
the lit downgoing, and under
soft masses of water the wrist
ribboned in weed, the hard sand,
the armored crabs in the clefts,
seaferns in the rock-knees,
deserted wood of killed galleys,
a gold coin in the sand,
the still stare
forever
of the upward eyes trapped under

the lost keel.
So from the boards in the sun
recall
that underwater,
and the lumber left, and the dead men,
and their names, and the ships' names,
and the dead faces.

Sea Changes

Not in one of its furies, but with absent care,
the slaty tide sucks bones of wood, spits them dry
on the sand; plasters a shell here, there
one derelict claw; brown weed ribbons (sea hair
waving submerged); pebble stuff, piled high.

Is it this thoughtful arranger, patting (now) a small splash
on sand, whose January angers boiled in whale-
battering shipless heaves of water, tall
in the gray gull-blown wind, to climb and crash
like a wet axe, and clobber and bruise our littoral?

Log it to commonplace that the sculpture of coast,
what sleeves and shapes the blue barrier either side,
is wild winter days blown monstrous, shaken slammed and lost;
with spelled calms, held water, carving slow and leaving uppermost
a decor of sea bones, shell spar net, displayed beyond high tide.

Not Happy Nature, Not Unhappy We

I do not fall upon the thorns of life.
I do not bleed.

Wading in sand on the western edge, we saw
the continent bordered with fishermen,
surf-blown about the feet, their Japanese
strong legs shoved into hip boots, standing
all in a lonely line, behind whose sentinel and seaward facing frieze the dunes
gave amorous escape to those hand-in-hand
couples that brushed the shrubs, and then were gone.
Our tactful eyes were also seaward. Some surprise
of light had torn the colors of the air,
or was it distance or illusion broke
the dragons of the skyscape Farallones
to fragments of mirage? Thunder-colored
on flame. Admirable. But the wind
blew in our bones.

And birds of the sea, what were they, all
necks and beaks, drove their bitter profiles across
the curtain of a storm where no storm was,
guided on rags of sea-lace, and went home,
wherever home can be for such.

                          And here, I thought
long afterward, watching the leafmen rake
and pile and burn the brown and bronze of Penn-
sylvanian oaks, and make their ordered lines of men

/ 11 /

make the slow pensive motions that men make at work,
here, as I thought again, we should have grieved
for our sad souls amid the spirit world
of broken water and grave birds. We were not sad
but only cold.
Weltschmerz today can be no private thing.
Not our hurt, but only the hurt of a world
with a worm in its axis, a rotten old ball
whose progress may at any moment begin to wobble
perceptibly.

        As for us, we sought to hide
behind the eucalyptus, whose abject leaves
thinned the water from the Pacific breeze
to drip on us.

        Huddling, no more in love
than for mere heat, we saw the fishermen
march homeward through the valley of the dunes
in profiles of wet hats and slanted poles
and solemn ordered lines of men at work.

And now in time of leafsmoke, ankle-deep
in crackled old bronze, where they rake and burn,
think how it was in smoke, spume, spindrift clouding
to haze the standing continental shapes
that we forgot to grieve
for our sad souls, and not the cracking world.

Note on the L & N

Bracketed by a diesel switcher and five
box cars before, and aft a red caboose,
with pistons pumping as if they were alive,
with eyeholes fixed ahead, cabhandles loose,
two old pacifics went
frogmarched to fate along the iron arc
that hooked the landscape to the edge of dark.

Dull on the wheels and ironed calm by time
the history of bright miles dies to the trip
of driving rods pushed from outside. They climb
in humped and prodded dead companionship
where the last curve is bent
and shapes them home. No more, in pride of steam,
will they thread out against the azure dream

of six o'clock on silver, past the sleep
of yards, the sleep of white grain towers, to raise
blue cities hours in future. Life is deep
dimmed in them, and their black is dull with days.
In a bewilderment
of motion they find aliens work their wheeled
stride to the scrapyard, and the ironmonger's field.

RMS Lusitania

Down under green,
under blown gray, white creaming
indigo across the collapse of slipping waterhills, thin
with wind hollowed through spray, gulls screaming,

under the cold still pool
of crosslit green that slabs the giant fidgeting skin of the
    world's ocean,
where water stilled, jelled, is nothing like water except
    to be cool,
and wears no color but color of silence after commotion;

there on the blind floor she has been lying
since the iron fish exploded in the heart,
since her short drama of dying,
sloped boats, hopeless swimmers, flame water steam shrieking
    her apart.

Big broken and black
she bulks there still in the gloom
with enormities of red keel, girded bridge and stack;
hulled gold (they said); paintings decor silver china;
    grace-ghosts of the stateroom, the dining room.

Lost? Saved? Sealed for judgment? Did you find
your islands there, your harbor and berth, green down
these miles, promised that day, that moment above in the sun,
    when your blind
and dying swimmers watched you drown?

Steam Crossing: Midwest

Grass dries brown between rails.
Weeds crowd up through concrete slabs. A few
strung wires slant. The grain tower
shapes a white tube on the blue.

The Wooden Implement Store is padlocked.
Boards slat bare in the sun. Through cracks
bent blades, shovels and plows, tool
handles cross in sepia gloom. The tracks

define the blank front of town. Far
at the crossing, cars, bright new bugs, pick
a dainty way between gate arms. A single truck
careens, lurches near, one thick

chocolate arm coiled in the window. From
blind trees, steam whistles. Wheels grow
noise on rails. The burly black
locomotive barrels into the straight, builds big, slow

breathing hard brakes by, jerking
a hundred hoppers. Thunder follows
fading with the caboose; withdraws.
Quiet sucks in as sky sharpens, hollows.

The sunball bronzes, sinks. Heat
blurs thinner. Scattered cars
pick at the crossing now. The street
goes gray. The sky is washed, ready for stars.

Arrangement In Nature

One stands, deep buckled into stones, who grudge
way, down into dark ground. Deep scored, brown
bole and waist buttress formality
of branch bent to salute coils swarming with sightless years
lost. Still in strength lurks somewhere
a curve here, there a shy bend of adolescence deprecates
but is absorbed in these mature manners. So stands he

and all eyes are all elsewhere. Circling the site
round hills recede, clouds turn improbable in blue
and distract, but elsewhere still again
curtseys willow grace, or nubile aspens, shy
but seeming ever within reach, beckon
to absolutely impossible communions; or nearer in April toss
the heads in flowers of apples, pretty confusion now
before pink grays (as belle fades all too fast
to fabulous beauty, past days dimmed in dowager);
as bushes whisper, and stir of green intimates
that all about
are false consents to marry, tremulous yes on every side
(and tendrils all golden to finger, see!).

But Two stands, half opposite, not unaware
of the courtesy in acknowledgment, male
to maiden and melting green. No warm in stare
here: irony guards tenderness: shoulder
modeled to half experience turns half away.
Gesture says nay.

There is no future. Yes, but deep
under, pushing, months are inch, below
cold stones, roots grope blind, know
block and deliberately recoil, then slow
push, past dirt bagged in water, bones
trickling, and grow
fingers: and nothing more, no seed here, no
mouth: it is not marriage, no.
Yet here, deep, past block
of boulder, buried mole, blind and slow
shall hard fingers interlock?

Romantic Landscape with Story

Drenched in wet silver, pale with olive and still
with flowers upon the folded hands of day
the garden at the bottom of the hill

sleeps in arrested expectation. Mail
dramatic on the outline of the rock
a black knight rides his armor down the trail

in quest of histories lived long ago.
Where are our amoureuses? Are they all gone?
But in the lyric valley, dreams below,

memory burns the banners of old nights;
the chimes of stars turn pale upon the hour;
and there, as gardens dawn, and as the lights

of twelve day-candles wink out one by one,
my love walks tenderly where cherubim
choir their rosalbas in the silver sun.

Despair in Seascape

Here is the fix: an hour of time crossed over
a mile of beach to hold disparate
materials, as dunes, boats,
assorted anatomies and almost any amount
of water.

          One end of a mile
anchors on those swings, pinwheels, and bannisters a mile
makes into toys; one end smudges off
into soft strokes, haze of dunes and undefined
limit of surf. On feet shoveling
the dry loose hills, on feet (the same) paddles
to smack the wet hard flat
of the afterwave, traverse, loop in, and hold
the scenes of which this mile is composite
in the sightless frame of an hour.

                    Or try.

                         Because
any here is elsewhere before you can pin
it to when; because the breaking, the broken, and to-break
wave sucks into itself and wipes
its shine off the sand before the sand
is through shining; because the child's
sea wall, slapped on as slime, is cement, is sand, is wet
no-shape and no-wall; so because
on this material symmetry all moves
except the color of the sand, all sounds
except the silence of the dunes.

/ 19 /

                          Or no? Because
seen gull, shell, leg, spade, chair
escape through holes in that gray envelope of nerve
we pull around them, will not stand and be
anything simple like dimensions?

                          The child
spading his bucket is that child you thought you knew
how to reshape and hang upon the mind,
and collapses without weight.

                          Far out, an arc
of marlin, jumping, hanging, clubbed like exclama-
tion points could never be believed
before gone and turned by memory into birds, about
whom nothing is improbable.

                          Even
a detail of nuns walking against the foam and gray
of breakers seems to fly like fragments
of those bird thoughts that haunt the changes of the sea.

All the most loved and vulgar knees and knobs,
angles of people, posts and piles, also specials
as marlin, nuns, blimps, storms
became as wingless, slipping in fragmentary space,
more gone when they were there than they are now.

Dufy, Grandma, or Alice should have painted
this poem I could not write.

        / 20 /

2

Omsk

Stands in the middle of a treeless plain.
In January, winds pile snow; in May,
sand. From the Ob by steamer, and by train
from Vladivostok, or by pony sleigh
from anywhere, it is accessible.
The streets are made of mud, the houses wood
(stone under construction). Educational
societies flourish. Industries include
the making of machinery and beer,
foodstuffs. And when, in 1917,
the army of the Bolsheviks drew near,
the town was full of western refugees,
who fled on east, and strewed the way between
with dead from cold, fear, hunger, and disease.

Ona

An Indian tribe, once in the interior
of Tierra del Fuego; giants, or akin
to giants; great hunters, and men of war.
Their chief food was the meat, their dress the skin
of the guanaco. Seldom did they sleep
in houses. They used hides to break the cold
out of the wind. They were concerned to keep
the Ona young subordinate to the old
by making tribal candidates go through
a rite of masks to learn theology,
then live alone two years, and so grow stout
and confident. They feared devils and knew
one supreme spirit. Ona mythology
is very rich. The tribe has now died out.

Onagraceae

A family of dicotyledon.
In Britain, the small herb Ludvigia
grows in damp pools, but in America
it is false loosestrife. Pollination
chiefly by bees and lepidoptera,
or when the flowers are pale and open on
the evening, as in evening primrose, one
may use nightflying insects. Clarkia
with epilobium hirsutum, known
as the great hairy willowherb, are still
to add. The flowers are regular in shape.
The New World breeds them in its temperate zone,
but tame oenothera biennis will
grow wild in Britain as a garden escape.

Hara-kiri

There are two kinds, compulsory and free.
A gracious note comes from the emperor;
with it a dagger. Friends and family
kneel in a formal circle on the floor.
Beside you kneels your second (Kaishaku).
You confess, are handed the dagger. This you put
below the waist, drive home, and draw it through
the stomach, ending with an upward cut,
while the Kaishaku swings his sword upon
your neck. This is the old, forced way, not now
performed. The other kind is often done
even today, but the book does not say how.
I gather that you are allowed to do
it your way, so long as the knife is pulled clear through.

(N. B. ALL information is derived from the edition of 1936)

Hirohito

Now reigning emperor of Japan, and son
of Emperor Taisho. He was visiting
in Europe when, in 1921,
Taisho retired from public life, leaving
his son established in the regency
for the next five years or a little more
(for this regime, *see* JAPAN: *History*).
Then Hirohito became emperor.
The new reign was officially designated
the period of Showa (Light and Peace),
and the Mikado blessed this period
with his own manifesto, circulated
through all the realm, and laying emphasis
on harmony at home and peace abroad.

Hiroshima

Fortunate in its lovely situation
beside the waters of the Inland Sea,
Hiroshima has raised its population
from about a hundred thousand (1903)
to a quarter of a million souls today.
The city stands on a small plain, between
hills and the islands scattered on the bay.
Its fame is partly due to the serene
and nearby presence of divine Bentin
on her small island, and to the belief
that she bestows an influence from heaven,
for she is god of radiance, and has been
adored by pilgrims, constantly.

                            The chief
temple dates from the year 587.

Hitler

Bavarian politician, Austrian
by birth. Once draughtsman, later editor.
His first putsch failed, but later he began
the N-S party. Versailles and the War
had left Germany sullen and embarrassed
by debts. So Hitler was successively
chancellor, dictator, führer, and at last
Reichs-Führer with supreme authority.
He has been violent against the Jews,
is charged with excesses in party strife,
has re-armed Germany and suppressed free news.
Hitler is said to lead a private life
both simple and sincere. He does not use
tobacco or liquor, and he has no wife.

Memoir Suggested by Recent Revivals: F. S. F.

One is to remember the way fragments of a rose
disintegrate to minor fragments when pressed in
a memory book
and how the identical and breathing rose would look
fastened against a twenty-year-old midnight with a formal pin.

One is to dim his eyes on photographs and read
them while the foxtrot toils on the victrola, scan
the personal poise
of little girls in dancing-school hair-ribbons, boys
in norfolk jackets. All look slightly boiled, but are admired American

specimens dehydrated from our ardent youth.
The brittle music opens and the night is kind,
as a live flower
intimately unrobing in a petal shower
strews all in white the chopping waters of the mind;

and May was miracle when all were wild and young,
and it is Mediterranean whose small tide-heaves
sea-comb the drifting hair
in summer glints of drowning Vega and Altair;
and it is northern autumn borrowed in a fall of oaken leaves.

The manikins. Were they stuffed dolls manipulated
by remote control to posture in the pose
of flesh and blood,
or is there fragrance in the air where these have stood?
I cannot judge between the book-pressed and the severed garden rose.

Voyage of Discovery: 1935

Shall we go on with it? Driving ever seaward?
Invisible wings outride this narrow passage.
We see towers golden on the sand. We hear sirens.

The foam flanks widen, the world is split obliquely
after the wind and wings have blessed the burden
of oars swept to the hammer beat no longer,

after the sails were scrapped and the trefoil blades
grind vaster trembling hulls forever forward,
after these and after, the same way always;

the water wrenched astern is a net of wishes,
epitaphs of next years, and the way ahead
tomorrows meeting mortality, imaged islands,

and left and right tomorrows that never happen,
and if you swing the helm and the rudder answers,
sleeve by arm they follow, and still are sidewise.

Maybe the yellow horns quiet the grave water
at Cherbourg, the Solent trodden circumspectly
by giants, the armor and huddle of spears, Manhattan,

San Salvador or Vineland, the northern break
of continent with ice, it hardly will matter.
It will have been a false hope. It will have been

barely the other side of the wings outriding.
They are there, the lovely abstractions, the ifs and maybes,
the forever beyond, the fixed and fugitive,

the not anywhere, the always elsewhere islands.
Shall we go on with it? Driving ever seaward,
the spoke turning and the next spoke turning with it?

A people's purpose is to build its own death,
to be impatient of its youth and remember
that youth completed as a bright grief lost to it,

and break its heart to be young again, and be older,
and build that age in bridges and guns and armor
and meet its death by turning over tomorrow.

It is useless and there is nothing else to do.
The way to recapture is to go ever onward.
It is the only way left though you die of it.

O ever sheathing and seeming always forward
drowned seeming in blue dimension and lost water,
the rocks seaward, the templed capes, the green shallows,

the bright slopes hillward; in your lakes the swans
as by the strand your ships lie ever quiet.
We came there never but remember dying.

Equations on a Triad

These three,
Faith, Hope, Charity,
if Hope is Hope and future is despair
in hope, and Faith is myth and memory,
if Charity is love and love is care,
these three,
memory
act and morality
are mirror, kiss, infinity.

Immediately there is a field where green is ripped
to thunderpulse in the bladefooted gallop of three
white horses. There is a green tree stripped
to the white heart, with iron in her side.
There is a small beach edged in April sea,
and three tall girls
with hair rinsed in the wind and naked eyes
walk down it one by one
as pale sun drifts the blondeur of their curls:

since memory is a dance caught at the ocean side
and hope a wounded tree
and love is a green field where horses run.

Or through the strings of brain and brain of sense
comb out, and purge,
and fish for innocent fingers; so submerge
the lucency of act; so alter tense,

let memory live idea again and what has been
be index of the still unseen
where, as the callous horns the hand of innocence,
the wound beneath is green.

Those were a morality of nature; these
are keys (can be my keys)
to read my text or pencil out in minor scope
three syntheses
in understanding: Myth, Love, the idiot Hope,
in the grandeur of syntax or the continent scale
of grammar, past present conditional,
love substantive and adjectival past,
and future hope at last
the deadly process of material.

New Homes

Here where la belle lay dreamy in the bois
dormant, carved in the slumbers of a thousand years,
the figures of our sleepless nights invade
under green choirs spring's sleeping incunabula.
So the barbarian beast now paws and tears,

gobbles and chews green splendors and gray boles
through gouge of ground, scooped underbrush, and murdered trees.
So the dark memory of the wood is made
a dream of brick to house a thousand souls
in parcels of split-level domesticities.

Where are the slopes that leafed and shaded young delights,
where is the sorrel, and the ferns where lost we stood,
the footpath through the bracken where we stopped and played,
except where still, disturbing wiser nights,
the angers of the forest mutter in our blood?

Night Shifts

From twelve to two the locomotives in
the yard were busy with noise, crumbled the dark
distance with motions of their rituals,
slammed, coupled, shunted, switched, unhooked, returned
to lines of boxcars dark and docile waiting,
and slammed and coupled.

                      In the miles of night
the brain, his base half under sleep, half bare
in the dry spells of the clock and the gray time,
rode in their iron music, sat the grooves
of benches, stared at posters, counted digits
of time tables, and through the dirty panes
heard the night dragons coughing in their sleep.

Who is this sideman who strides through the gray
pulling me on a string, whose purpose wheels
my feet down years of rails and winter streets,
who builds my brains with cities never seen,
for whom I am a rag, a sponge to squeeze
for drops of lyric image, at whose slant
I am a paper in the wind,

                  and in
whose night, when the rain dries, the locomotives
bang their iron sonatas on no sleep?

Half white half gray, sunk to the neck in slumbers,
the bare mind dries in the wind as rain
has dried on stone and leaf, and down the miles
of winter dark my sideman slams and hooks,
shunts and uncouples dark and docile boxcars
all the gray times between, from twelve to two.

The Freighters

We watched the freighters and their classic brows opposed
to ocean on the pale Saint Lawrence waterway
solemnly crease, unsmoothe, and harrow the blue calms
and ride their masts to where the hulls squared slowly,
loomed through the gray
sails at the skin of the sightline, and were gone.

How far, we thought, between the continental slabs,
shall these calm edges stick and twist in the gray
tempers and the slub of the foamy stuff, each
caught as a kestrel fights the air with mere
strength to stay
the world below his struggle of wind and wing.

With such thoughts—no more than an antique legend of men drowned
in the gloom of memory—we outraged the v-shape and the cool wake
        that pulls
the swan's progress of slow freighters riding
their masts in spells of silence to the edge of sight
past where the hulls
grew square and big among the gray sails, and were gone.

Dry Light from Pylos

𐀳 𐀷⊕ ✲ 𐀁   𐀐 ≡ 𐀸   𐀃 𐀳 = 𐀸   𐀃 𐀺 - 𐀸   𐀁 𐀸

1

They come scratched on small clay slabs, from immemorial
stony places; contain obvious numerals; signs
for commodities, things, persons; and syllable
marks, now solved. They run to very few lines.

The fond eye can see a pitchfork, brush, or rake,
a handled basket or an anchored heart,
a butterfly, a four-candled birthday cake,
or proper heroics, chariot, throne, axe, dart.

What is in fact the woman-sign may become,
to the imaginative, a close-girt
Minoan lady with enforced bosom.
The man-sign, much like, has crossed legs, no skirt.

But these are ideograms. The syllabary
offers for *pu* a graceful animal,
while *da, ro, pa,* and *to* among them vary
the patterns of the cross; and almost all

make language now, deciphered to a kind
of Greek. Contents: sheer fact; inventory,
lists, and accounts of work. You will not find
heroic action, myths, or poetry.

2

Reading from left to right, the row begins
with a five-syllable word which seems to spell
a-ra-ka-te-ja: spinner, one who spins?
The woman-sign follows, with a numeral

tally, thirty-seven. Then the basket, then
a square tripod; so, *ko-wa;* it will mean
girls. There are twenty-six. Then *ko* again
with a different tripod. *Ko-wo.* Boys. Sixteen.

Last stands a sign, a sort of debased C.
It means some kind of measure, used for food,
grain, drink, or total diet, which will be
something quite basic, and not specially good.

Thirty-seven workers with their woman-sign
and fatherless girls and boys on patient feet
stand there forever waiting in a line
for whatever they are to be given to eat.

Waiting for the Barbarians

From the Greek of Constantine Cavafis
(Konstantinos Kabaphes, 1863-1933)

Why are we all assembled and waiting in the market place?

It is the barbarians; they will be here today.

Why is there nothing being done in the senate house?
Why are the senators in session but are not passing laws?

Because the barbarians are coming today.
Why should the senators make laws any more?
The barbarians will make the laws when they get here.

Why has our emperor got up so early
and sits there at the biggest gate of the city
high on his throne, in state, and with his crown on?

Because the barbarians are coming today
and the emperor is waiting to receive them
and their general. And he has even made ready
a parchment to present them, and thereon
he has written many names and many titles.

Why have our two consuls and our praetors
come out today in their red embroidered togas?
Why have they put on their bracelets with all those amethysts

and rings shining with the glitter of emeralds?
Why will they carry their precious staves today
which are decorated with figures of gold and silver?

Because the barbarians are coming today
and things like that impress the barbarians.

Why do our good orators not put in any appearance
and make public speeches and do what they generally do?

Because the barbarians are coming today
and they get bored with eloquent public speeches.

Why is everybody beginning to be so uneasy?
Why so disordered? (See how grave all the faces
have become!) Why do the streets and squares empty so quickly,
and they are all anxiously going home to their houses?

Because it is night, and the barbarians have not got here,
and some people have come in from the frontier
and say that there aren't any more barbarians.

What are we going to do now without the barbarians?
In their way, those people, they were a solution.

Loutsa Beach

Here, where the pillion riders with their bucks
sprawl in the pineshade, and the oleanders grow
red on the ruins of a house, and boys in trucks
ride from the factories to swarm the beach below,
the Nazis' squat pillbox
desperately defends the coast from nothing at all
but wind and water piling blue on the sea wall.

What thins the sun upon our backs is here
and with us, and we brought it with us, and assume
the shadow like a towel across our shoulders, peer
backward in haste. The giant slept in the next room
last night. This is the fear
that dried upon the wind after the Persian bones
were shucked in holes and sunken under tons of stones.

July and banners of the blown coast wheel
stormily up to dare the northeast and the night
dimmed in the cities of our brain, burst in a peal
of brass and bravery. But what makes the wind so bright
is still that thin, that real
terror that turned the Germans green and made them break
a house apart to guard what no one wished to take.

The Winter Story

Now on his bare bright pole, and wheeled with ice,
our balanced blue and brown and white partitioned ball
spins out of time
complete into time born, as in a winter stall
between the animals a new child cries
waked here at midnight on the chime.

And beat of angels' wings, slow and immense,
ponderously disturbs the far-dropped atmosphere
where space is blue,
and lonely kings from their cold towers assemble here
with shepherds out of stony fields, with citizens
in furred gowns, and with me and you.

Airwalk of angels, riding kings, and people,
shepherds, with bearded burghers and bland servants, come
to Bethlehem
as the world's music rings her children home
in chains of bell-notes breaking from the steeple
on us, who take our place with them.

Antiphonal

We have made the stone speak, featured the clay.
We have sculptured in gilt close curls over the ears
to carve ever a mask, ever a moving silence,
in even the inked word and the brain's web limning
a sign, graph, idea;
as who handle water's weight, basket the wind
(in the songs, in stone, paint moves over the paint)
deflect elsewhere the model, other the throat surrendered,
and turning the live flesh on the eyes' screen, mirror
a doll there, a dream.

We can mark the words' sound, ear to the beat
of the lips in their speech bent, pore over the scrolls;
we watch and admire, give you our eyes and voices,
and know the design spun is immense and important;
we hear, hush, obey;
but the meaning drowns in sense, eyes into eyes.
For your wounds we have pity, hands, water and oil,
adoring the deed, caught with the riding splendor
and using the male force to our own need measuring
propound there delight.

Koré is Persephone and the moon really
is Artemis and Koré, Ashtaroth is Rapunzel
blanched in the milky moon, princess in the window
leaning on white elbows is also Koré
and Danaë drowning in gold is
Koré and Persephone, and they knew properly

ritual and figure, smile in wood and they danced to it:
symbol that means nothing, girl in the cornfield
standing in gold tassels whom once we waved to
and kissed her and knew in August.

Logic is abstraction and it is the stuff really
informing the need for action, action is the mind wearing
substance to stir substance. Accidents are female,
death, sex, and hunger. But your own hot god is
the sunflare on whom actual girls are
incident. We know it, adore you properly,
paraphrase and statue, eyes in stone and they painted them,
figure that is all meaning, man at the stars' edge
leaning beyond mystery that once touched us
and lived, through us, idea.

We would have known really and forever
(if we could have stayed, if we could have stayed)
Rapunzel to make you and the idea
burn single down the calendar, if
there had been no wars
and no argument.
We wear across our throats the flower and the picture.

We understand really and admiring
(if you had waited, if you had waited)
accept and yield in the shadow of ideas
one thing meaning what you wish, if
we may keep our moon
and our mysteries
and be (time into time) your image and memory.

Epigraphical Note

They arranged what was left and put it away.
Lysidice was young enough to lie alone.
Her house and the bones of her house were there to stay.
We read, from the incised stone:

I tell those who come here: there shall be a curse
on him who shall handle, dirty, or defile
me and my image, or dislocate, or force,
or shatter, obliterate, remove anything. May God not smile

on him, but smite him with terror of the eyes, distress
his wits and body with fever chills itch blight;
may he not tread ground nor sail water; die childless;
go cold in the sun and blind in daylight.

And so forth. Lysidice died and meant to stay dead.
She had stood in the sun. She had loved poetry
and truth, as surely as she was sweet and young, she said.
She did not want to die. Now let her be.

They excavated, intensely loving, collected
the fragments, read her, and sorted her in a sieve.
She is now scientifically resurrected,
and these bones live.

Monumental

In Schönbrunn stands a hunk of statuary.
Slabs of old armor no one ever wore
in any age, dog-Greek-cum-Latin, vary
the martial attitude around a core
of marble nonsense. So they stuff with blanks
the shirts of Mars. Does opposite Venus drape
a featureless anatomy, and thanks
to new look mitigate her lack of shape?
So obvious my myth. Not brawn of shoulder
as never bulging bust, not even bone
and garbage once humanity can moulder
in this preposterous pinnacle of stone.
Nor Mars incarnate nor his Cytherea
can populate a petrified idea.

Rise and Shine

At the big trumpet we must all put on
our dentures, tie old strings to knees, adjust
shank upon socket, wig to cranium, bust
on ribbed architrave, fastidiously don
our properties, and blink to face the sun.
Farewell, dream-image cankered in our dust,
and sweets shrunk in the brain, farewell, we trust.
Uprise, o fragment brethren. We have won.
For, halleluia, these dry graves are torn.
Thin bugles crash the valley of our bones
to rock the vultures wide away and scare
the griffin from his precipice; as, worn
and damp, we crawl like grubs from under stones
to scarf our loves in paradisial air.

The Brink

They said: When we came into those seas, the mast peak
shot leaves; the wood grew, groaning; the air was
sticky with grapes. That musing iron beak
bit seas no longer, but like a scythe in grass

was hushed. About then world's end was our lee shore.
And we believe, when stack and siren bloom,
and doubled left and right these wake-wings flower
astern into perdition and the gloom

on the world's eyes. Vines strangle every spar.
The oars broke into serpents in our hands.
We knew those islands, and the end not far.
And now the captain's eyes are bronze; a man's

feet petrify. The wood weeps. Silver and glass
branch into rose and shoulder; willows weave,
are arms. Below, the water turns to grass.
Beyond, those island bells. And we believe.

Invictus

If we can only go on saying what we must go on
saying; if our voice is mournful monotony, as rain insists
all dripping night; if we protest too much the malevolence

of our dirty-gray intentions and our morning-afters of lovemaking,
we are not necessarily waste or weary; we may still be
the bat boy who made the team, the third son who was stupid.

We have passed the dry tree and said goodbye to the thorn on the rock.
We waded the smashed green thunder of the river that forbids
hope forever. We have not found the white poplar nor the water

of memory, but we are still walking. While ant lugs
home the twenty times his size slain bug, while dung beetle
wrestles his intolerable Atlas ball, while son

of a gun of a spider climbs up the water spout in the rain's face,
bless our heroics, please. I said we passed, then lost, certain
      landmarks
in the shouldering dark; the white rock, the orange tree, and the
      voices,

and we are still walking where we must walk and because we must go
on walking, and having passed much more than this we have forgiven
and thrown away the bitterthin of selbstmord longed for through rain.

A smashed toy or eyes given elsewhere made us passionate
for water of oblivion once, but we crossed over Lethe
and started up the other side of the valley. The rockline escapes

backward as we climb, and what is beyond eludes, invisible
always behind a slowly reeling wall. But is there (we knew this
bathing by bare rock half inside the cold mountain)

and is a thing in itself, positive, peremptory,
not in the shadow of a borrowed grace, not to be endured
for the sake of something else. Nor cross called us,

nor moon's obelisk, snake, moth-urn of dead spirits, bull god
drowned god hanged god. Nothing. No god. But inside
the furious anatomy we fought, with a sword that could not

imaginably cut anything, the invasion of shadows. We passed
the sad tree, and the rock, the well of indifference, the night
     shaken
by the wings of bats, and in desolate morning cross over and climb to

a shelf-rock half way up the other side of the valley.

Hercules at the Crossroads

Through drenched grass, dawn unmisting, the April day's
prime hour, to a place where a spring comes cold in the shadow
        of poplar trees
and the cross-arms of the pounded road branch, two ways,
young Hercules
trudged, singing the morning up. And there in the shade
two girls waited him. She of the left-hand fork stood pale
and sweet, in a flowered dress, and smiled with made
lips, and allured him with a blue gaze, and sidled forward to
        hail

her hero. "Hercules. Here your way lies, my way. Here.
Take my hand, I will show you, but see how temperate, gentle
        and green
it goes. So shall your dearest life go with your hand in mine.
        Never fear,
I shall not leave you. Between
here and your days' end think nothing but cool progress, soft-
        soled
walking, sleep for hours, blithe company, agemates outwrestled,
        girls—yes, creamy legs, blond
looks; long nights of shorn white rosefall; for sedate age,
        goods and gold;
green sinews, honors lightly lifted, good memories. Look not
        beyond.

This is real." She ended, down-lashed, demure. And presently
        now, she

of the right-hand way came forward, queenly and sober, and by no
    means
repellent with her dusky plaits and grave eyes, and told him: "See
where your way leans
to the rock-base and the skinny thorn, the dry of the gorge where
    crickets
buzz through bones in bare sun and the big animals move in the night.
Haul up the stony grades day by day and scratch for sleep in the
    thickets.
Dry bread, strong food, scant water. Furthermore, you will have to
    fight

the hazards that fester our ways. The coarse footpad, ruffian,
    grifter, wizard and phony
shall test your nerve and brain, gristle and grip. Your pace will be
    slow,
your nights dogged and bare, days thin, and the trail stony.
I shall not go
with you. You are alone. Good luck and good bye."
    Hercules
stood footlocked and black with doubt, brow bent;
then chose, turned right, and stepped out of the poplar trees.
His eye slid once to the left. He waved and went.

Now here began a succession of sick and disastrous years
for the tough, the greedy, the cruel and sly of the world, here began
a most pitiable outcry, thumping and struggle as he laid them all by
    the ears.
The strenuous little man

/ 56 /

who fought from grinning helm with spear or bare with his bones, club,
    wrenched broad boles,
mashed snake heads, speared pounded butted or strangled lion and bull,
outsize pig, giant and ogre, and the monsters crawled away and hid in
    their holes.
Much done. But a thin and ragged life. Who has told how scarred and
    twisted, how pitiful

and used, the hero who walked the grand peaks in the end of his time?
A sad strong man, remembering every fight
and harsh from sour triumphs, fear and sickness, the gift of his
    prime,
the bare night
alone in the slum of the mind, the inward niggle of doubt.
Had he chosen right at the fork of the ways? Was it worth
the beating it took to pacify and set right a world torn inside out,
and fight his way to being the best man on earth?

This is a moral and momentous story I tell.
Here is the Y-shape of tragic choice, Hecate's fork, our sprung
    three-piece cross;
the trails to heaven and hell.
Yes, but which is which? The philosopher's gloss
I give you is one way of the fable, for the refined spirits
to read and ponder. Crasser souls will have it that Hercules
never was lonely. He was a cram-eater, a lap-handling bully boy.
    Doubtless with merits
but much rewarded. We disagree. Now back to my scene at the trees.

The dark girl had told him nothing whatever about any reward.

It is true, he is chapeled with St. Demetrius and St. George, a
        hero in glory
with angelic sword.
He is said also to have loved many lovelies along the way, but this
        will not accord with our story.
The somber she of the right was gone from his life.
But brute work captures charms and heroes sometimes land in the lush.
        Did he ever see his little friend
in the flowered skirt again? Find her waiting after all at a last
        crossroad and make her his wife?
I do not know. But it seems established Hercules married well at the
        fiction's end.

Tudor Portrait

Brusque shoulders and bluff beard,
hated, caressed, and feared,
hornbeam-and-hickory-hard,
gartered and starred,

in slash and puff complete
he stands, all male six feet
and fourteen stone of him,
bulky and trim

astride the austere hall,
big brute divinity,
to master from his wall
Christ Church and Trinity.

Saint, devil, ape, or man?
Soul perfect shaped or maimed?
Human or God's the plan
that left him (named

Defender of the Faith)
to win at point of death
his bitter and his brief
uncouth belief?

Manwolf loose on the land,
reformer with red hand,
verse maker, lout with Latin,
savage in satin;

coarse hulk of glory stopped
on the last bed of all beds
in a dream circle of lopped
and leering heads

from gross and glittering past,
saw he yet at the last
through the brain's breaking screen
what he had been:

monks' bane, so faith shall flower;
strong king, so kings shall cease;
brute, that there be no war
on earth, but peace?

So judge. But what he saw
shows nothing in jowled jaw
where, stiff astride the wall
of the harsh hall

he built, gaudy and grand
in sceptre, star, and crown,
on strong new worlds he planned
the king looks down.

Barbara

(Young Jemmy Grove on his deathbed lay)

If I am to be judged and sit apart
in scarlet shame
to wear the favors of my lovely name
upon an iron heart,
I do not know
what I was meant to be
nor why I go
as cruel Barbara, rung home and led
by bells to my cold bed;

since, though I drag my depths for some drowned, dim,
and perished thought
lit with the smiles and eyes they think I ought
to have surrendered him,
I find no love
I was supposed to know
for Jemmy Grove,
nor why his love for me should make me say
that I shall die today

for my true love for his true love that died
on a sick bed
for me, Barbara, cursed with rhymes and led
by bells, in scarlet pride,
to lie alone
without the power to change
on my gravestone
the legend of the lies that shall be said
of me when I am dead.

/ 61 /

The Wounded

"The Bomb is the Biggest Thing in our Life"

"Nous sommes trahis"

1

A ball of dishonor swims in the dark of moons.
We are a corporation of treasonable dust, and our dust
nurses death by fire in the pit of her own loins.
Oh Aristotle, flower lives, ape moves, but man is reasonable.
Therefore we are betrayed;
and what is decay in my bones, tetanus in my heel, copperhead
     in my path, but this
which is silver in singing and witty grace of iron in speech
and a ceremony of stars in the mind's cold contemplation;
which is formal sweetness of calculus and grammar?
What that is not lovely
brought us to this shame, ulcered our heel, pounded the
     powder
of our probable holocaust and terminal Bikini?
And where, if a hand shall lift us
at last from the foaming pit and we win the islands,
shall that be found which shall incorporate our salvation,
if not small, folded, writhing
deep hearted in the ulcer?

2

On his rock, Philoctetes,
poking the scum at the beach break,

a crippled crow of a man, watched wings
circle expectant
of meat, flesh of my flesh crawling on the bones' weariness.
Contemplating his foot,
Philoctetes, myth man and symbol,
thus to self: My blue mirror,
pale platter of argent and azure,
scurf-rimmed to the bend of dirt and dishonor,
swarms under slime the glitter of fish, green hair of the
      mermaid
undine idea sublucent.
Haze lipping the hard horizon
hoods large lovely men who must choke on large notions:
a fort to burn, a pretty prince to shoot down.
They have dust to lick, knees to double before all this is ended.
No, this smelly bulk is not crow's meat, no rag of feathers.

Look at yourself, Philoctetes.
Wrong stains the heart of nobility:
is answered:
light builds in the wound.
Behold, as the lipped fang-cut reeks in the white foot,
and the huge grace and stateliness of muscle is bitten
to a loop of blubbering pain: yet I cuddle the stock to my
      cheek
and pick a fall of wings out of the shining circle.
I tell a man to go and he goes. I tell one
to stay and he stays. In the light of a moonlong check and
      recoil
my corruption is starred in silver.

/ 63 /

At the scum of the sea break squatting in the ooze I,
    Philoctetes,
suck the dry sherds of my honor.

            3

We, who were betrayed
by the angels rinsed in the secrecy of our blood, swept in the
    loins' liquid,
how shall we tear our crippled meat free from the rock of
    starvation?
Turn, supplicate the wounded.
Their myth: a sky screaming wings, the gray towers huge in a
    penitence of water.
Their salvation: the mercy of the wrong wind, no moon no glory.
Their character in action: the painted helmets flowers alive in
    the jungle flowers
and a darkness hairy with metaphysical apes.
Turn to Benteen and Reno on the hill swept in the riding terror,
to Mallory and Irvine on the last ledge's escape in a thin
    sky.
And when the forlorn are as kings among men and the large
    men are forgiven,
and the dagger is a scalpel of mercy,
may the wound sleep at last in the heel; the bomb die.

The Bridge at Arta

Freely translated from the Modern Greek (Anonymous)

There were master masons forty-five
    there by the water's edge,
and sixty apprentices worked with them
    to build the Arta bridge.

All day they would work to build it.
    Each evening it would fall.
Mourned then the master masons
    and their apprentices all:

"Useless the work we waste on this
    and vain the toil of our hands.
All day we strive to build the bridge,
    in the evening nothing stands."

With that there came a little bird
    and across the river flew.
It did not sing the way birds sing
    nor as the swallows do.
When it sang it spoke in a human voice
    and told them what it knew.

"Unless you kill a human soul
    your bridge will never stand,
but you must not kill an orphan child
    nor a stranger in the land.

But there is the master mason's wife,
    and she is sweet as a rose.
Let her come slow, let her come swift,
    to see how your work goes."

The master mason heard him speak
    and death was in what he heard.
He thought upon his little light wife
    and spoke his thought to the bird:

"Late must she rise, late must she dress.
    late must she take her way,
late must she come to the Arta bridge
    to see what we do today."
But the little bird paid him no heed
    but said what it wished to say:

"Rise swift, my dear, dress swift, my dear,
    and swiftly take your way,
and swiftly come to the Arta bridge
    to see what they do today."

They saw her come down the white road.
    They saw the way she took.
The master mason watched her come.
    The heart inside him broke.
From far away she greeted them,
    from close at hand she spoke:

"Good health to you, joy be with you,
    each master and every lad;
but what ails the master mason,
    and why is he so sad?"

"Oh, it is my ring that I have dropped
    inside the foremost pier,
and who will go down and who will stay down
    and fetch it to me here?"

"Now master, I will fetch the ring.
    You shall not be so crossed.
For I will go down and I will stay down
    till I find the ring you lost."

She scarce had gone down to the water side
    and scarce stood within the pier
when "Pull up the rope," she cried to him,
    "pull up the rope, my dear,
for I have searched through all this place,
    and I find nothing here."

Then one threw rubble and one threw lime
    on where she stood below,
but the master mason took a great stone,
    lifted, and let it go.

"Now a curse upon the fate of me
    and mine, for it was hard.
There were three of us who were sisters once
    and the three of us were ill starred.

One sister was killed for the Danube bridge
    and one the Euphrates slew.
Now here beneath the Arta bridge
    I meet my own death too.

Then as the leaves of the walnut tree
    are shaken and drift down,
so let this bridge be shaken, and they
    who cross it tumble and drown."

"Now speak a different curse, my sweet,
    and put the old curse by
or you might curse your only brother
    and he might cross and die."

Then she changed her words, she changed her curse,
    all for her brother's sake.
"When the wild mountains tremble
    let this bridge tremble and break.

Let those who cross fall in and drown
    when the wild birds fall from the sky,
for the sake of my brother in a far land
    that he may not cross and die."

Glaukos

Inward your black globe crumbles wearily.
Lean inward past the sinew of the heart.
Far underneath red springs of breathing see
the sober fabrication break apart.

And you have laid aside your yellow hair,
models of motion that were hands are gone
and the free arms and surfaces that wear
tints like a change are dropping one by one.

Stand in the white square of the centre, shed
leaf after leaf the dwellers in your mind
stirred backward whence the green cutwater spread
two ruins wincing down the ways behind.

A debris of bright accidents is laid
about your feet, and in the mediate space
circle your form naked as it was made
and turned toward its own symbol, face to face.

He stands. The prints of shells are in his beard,
the grave arms tasseling green weed that drips
the ooze salt to his feet; the hands are smeared
with pulp; the gray scurf stiffens on his lips.

Yet for your presence light begins to glow
red like a lamp for Mary, and the stone
is shriven of excrescence. Slow and slow
the fragments drop. The figure stands alone.

/ 69 /

The ocean kept him, where Atlantis near
rippled its towers of stone across the gloom
of water falling quiet. He is here.
The sea drains moaning from this shuttered room,

the shells and weed upon the noise, to leave
the stone as live as when the quarry broke
unbosoming his contour. Do not grieve.
Distance was littered in your eyes. You woke

to meet your lover rising from the sea
on the green stairway winding to the sun
between your shadow and your heart. Let be.
Distance has died between, and you are one.

Leilah

From the French of Leconte de Lisle

Sound of wingbeat, murmur of running springs, have fled
the air. The sun, a cinder, swims across the gay
grass, and with his thief's beak the furtive bengalee
drinks the rich juice of mangoes colored as if they bled
gold. In the king's close, where mulberries ripen red
under bare sky, from which all color has burned away,
Leilah, rosy and languid in the heat of day,
shuts deep-lashed eyes. Branch shade is dark about her head.
Her jewelled forehead leans on one delightful arm.
The amber of her bare foot colors soft and warm
the pearled film of her tiny shoe. She dreams apart,
and smiles upon her dreaming of how lovers meet,
like some fruit grown deep colored, passionate and sweet,
that makes the mouth's desire a lightness in the heart.

Pandora

Two o'clock. The house hums with silence, save
where time ticks in the person of the clock
beside the stair, no more than a dry pulse
held in a vein of amber.

                 Now she comes
alone and barefoot down the stair, and holds
the stopper to the vase she carries. All
that changes through the beating heart of this
midsummer afternoon, goes where her feet
go, and as shadow, over the sunned grass
to where the cool of midnight is forever
trapped in green leaves and tunneled over stones.
She has not looked behind, and now she looks
and sees nothing but summer in the sun,
and takes the stopper from the vase.

                     Nothing
comes out. She waits, and with her pulse the world
fails in its perfect wheel of stride. What came
out was not seen. It was the time of change,
and not the ripple on the waterskin,
and not the wind that moves the ripple, not
the bent plash where the ripple swims ashore,
but only the three corners of the way
wind is to ripple, ripple is to wind,
and both are to the water's edge, and edge
is merged with wind and ripple in one still
and solemn fact. Who can see fact? She knows

no time of change; but sudden in the blue
a bolt unpins, as in a downward blur
of swallows, what sweet gray imaginings
rinse from the color of behind your eyes
in love's aftersleep. Green foils shudder. Roots
draw in.

        For this, who shall not stand and watch
the beak nod in the rainbow spray of strange
blues, and the smoke of burning houses light
his yesterdays? Who shall not raise from mist
of memory those windows where the film
of pearl is figure? Or who will not leave
his bones to mark the night, and rendezvous
with helm-winged seeds to ride the sky and face
forgiveness in the end of all his days.

Life has begun. This was the act of death.
The penalty of tumult. Here the lines
of shatter in a glass grow big and make
a cloud of fission that will never rain
its life away and die.

        Garden goodbye.

She rises and takes up the empty vase.
The gold of summer is a robe to cowl
her quiet's measure as she tiptoes back
to where the clock, dead sentry, lets her pass,
and where her husband slept in the cool room
and does not know the world where he will wake
is all a world away from where he slept.

Demeter in the Fields

Demeter in the fields walks down the green
slopes, by the grooves of springs and in the grass
of watercourses and the cottonwoods
that cloud and mark the long slant of the valley
on the piled silt of mythic river kings.
This land, spelled in the legends of its names,
dreaming as in a bell of glass at noon,
or closed beneath Orion in the sky
fixed striding, where the daughters of the dove
shine on the bull's black shoulder, and the bear
wheels her bright dipper on the polar star,
this land is hers, who wades in the grain, who turns
the colors of the sloping soil and sees
brown changed to green in May and green to gold
in June.

       This is the goddess of the grain
who by the sea at the horns of rock and by
the time of air burned into day's end, stood
to curse the world with salt, for Death and the Maiden,
for laps of flowers and the young hair so seized
and raped; for her lost daughter in the ground.
But this was marriage and the seeding of years.
The hairy god and his bright virgin keep
the subterranean ritual, and their loins
swarm up in gold and children of the corn,
and on these slopes Demeter of the rocks,

the mother, centered in a trinity,
walks softly as the wings of her folded hands
cradle a blessing on the field of pain.

She is the noon siren sleep. She gives
love under lattices while the clock nods
and blood hums in its drain. She is the sense
of separation and surrender, she
the drowsy sphinx of summer, in whose lens
the serpent and the dove combine to burn.
Her unintelligible magic swims
across the preening eyes of men and girls
adaze along the tawny heaves of fields.

Now in the young time of the year they come
to cut the bronzed and bearded heads of wheat,
stack the lopped manes in golden walls, and blow
the dusty yield of summer into bread,
then homeward, blade on shoulder, hand in hand,
walk slow between the piles of the year's wealth
past the white chapels mounded on the hills
crossed with the arms of Christ, and consecrate
to Mary Panaghía and her saints,
to Isis, Ashtaroth, and the blood of the moon,
to female earth, Demeter in the fields.

White Harbor

Slow clouds are bells
in blue drowned
and sleep and die
with cold shells
as underground
wells, and lie
in shattered light
deep blue down.

Walls were white
if walls were,
by golden fringe
on waterblue
sea shawl.
But sands blur
build, winds push
slowly through
ruin, where wall
went.

    Bend back
from water eyes'
asking sweep
and goldenslack
ground lies
in lizard sleep.

Seaward and moored
in jelled blue

the keelboard
dreams true
dreams.

That mound, that not natural hill, heaved, under
piled in drifts of rubbling generations, that earthmound
is it.

Here at the doubled cross, seaward and landward, one arm
of the cross breaking Asia open, one the blue sheer of the Cyprus
main, they built it, or rather not they, or not built, but the moun-
ding started, in dawn utensils being handled, in squatting
by night to the huddle of sociability, in day by day the convergence
of casual ways backfolded on a circle near water and a piling
city begun.

(In night, in the dark of the mother, uncoils
through soft struggle what will be shining, brainflower
that bursts: the manners that make courts, sagacity of the markets:
the little ceremonials of uprise and the bath, food broken
and tasted with others who taste and break food: the small and
    infinitely
sweet ceremonials of goodnight: and dark: and light: involved
in absolutely ordinary day-things: and dark again, golden
monotony of routine when the world was golden.)

What need pulled the indrift of outlanders on this core
of peoply warmth: and who; it stays uncertain, if only
a serviceable harbor, pale sheet for ships' self-admiration
and land complacent along the sweet bend of the shore. At least

it was not protection, no fat fort to hulk its frown
of military indignation black on its people. This was
entirely a bourgeois proposition. It meant peace.

Islands always meant more than islands: yours
or mine. As on the baked macadam summerhaze
runs ripple of water that is not there, siren allures
seafarer, sand is wells; as memory drowns our days
in stations of the past; as stars of hope
pick out the winter sky that waits, to mark
our pale procession down the western slope
where gone-before-us gibbers in the dark.
Islands are always elsewhere

as for
the bleak farmer who weathered a hillside of stones, with his
lawsuits and his calendars of days: his steading
dropped away from the cream and blue, the drenched in danger
and desirable swan's way, gull's way, wheel and plunge of the
    merchant
ship. At the intersection in midstone, neither blessed with
a shiver of breezes in August blaze, nor sunlight to unsharpen
wounds against winter: lost in the wheels of time worn out
the days of sun, and man and god considerate, lost alike in the fog
of a northern channel sundance of promise to come. In the fixed
    intersection
of the positively worst time at the absolutely worst place, he sang out
the days of glimmering graces, saw islands but could not name them,
sang out the graces across the slopes of hastening hillsides,
and night revolved in over the scaurs, its color iron

as a grumpy Venus gathered against her sides still golden
attendant cherubs, and trailed them off to simper in sunlier
climates.

To him, islands immerse in death, and dead men
move magnificent, converse with stately and tall
gestures about nothing in particular, or stride in procession
of brainless grace. Here all men are kings, except that
no men are men.

But there
dredge deep down
in the sand's pile
gold under lit blue,
sludge of the Nile
rinsed clean as bone
and north dragged
glims through
where pale lateen
caught the sky's
drench, between
brown arms
and brown eyes,
where days slipped
and laughter bubbled
under starburnt
arch black above
where dim nudes troubled
the waters

(not as in lotus, asphodel, aquamarine
projections of the always-gone, the neverseen
escape of memory through the flights of time-between)

    in the mound above
    find them, break
    the noon sleep,
    past block and stone
    dig down,
    dig deep.

Slowly, and sober with method, pick at first
and spade hack out the holes. Round of a vase
shoulder, or sleeping pot, stir in the torn
earth, and emerge; or half arc of a well;
the angle of a bastion or a drain.
Now the coarse iron checks, and knives suggest
away the mould that clings upon, or fingers
fiddle with, these fragilities.

                Such mulled
and such disturbed and fragmentary clots
of pattern mean a morning of the world.
When the last spade has turned, and all the men
gone home; the gold wiped and the splintered clay
glued up; the floors scrubbed bare and labeled, pots
arranged to smile from prim order through glass,
symbols pick out in points of light their years,
and Eden is a fossil in July.

    / 83 /

A salve jar is a crucible to make
an ordinary nine o'clock upon
the lips of no extraordinary girl
into a blush, a stammer of amaze
and a wild pulse under bland moons, to hold
as guard against tomorrow and the years
remembered in a mirror.

                    On a dish
chariots and lions, showier, hold the pride
of man's desire, for one in whom no show
was worth the pride and loss.

                        And where they built
their careful and their monumental drains,
smile we at material civic self-importance
that makes their streets and houses other than
sties bleared obscene with dung and slops and flies.
Politic, they guarded skin. No thump of nailed
in bronze Assyrian mace was knotted to
the habit of their hands. (The tissue's schemes
are in their letterclay.) They played it safe
between the looming beetle and the wolf.
A room where secretaries bent might mean
lines of thought twisted into strings, to bind
tissues of fierce desires in sheaves of peace.

This is the suburb, the grocery, the garden
next door. Her stars are ours. Her blood beats to
our pulse.

    / 84 /

We own, we sign to and acknowledge
the symbols lying near.
A hoard of golden coins. A pile of swords.

Materially elsewhere, mine in strand
of hair so thinly binding bone on bone, o land
forgotten of your gods, dead in the sand.

Green go they in their brief sun. The broken edges of winter
are iron hooping their horizon's wheel. For the northward water
bitterblue boils, and the hordes stir swarming. Skullfine, arrogant,
limblank; seeing the loveliness shaped in a sword; their blond locks
swept in battlewind; their girls golden, cleanstepping, iceblue
in the long eyes; their babies steeled in cold springs; the destroyers
move.

      Green go our people, the sunlight tender about them,
young, not long to live. The bearded hawk of the desert,
the hideous vulture, move and follow. Go gay, my people,
in late afternoon. South of your feet that flitter so lightly
crawl, suspicious with gods, the dark hordes that infect the desert's
thin encounter with trees and the green crescent.

                         Fanatics
fidget with knives, they the skilled in despair, the learned
in not, in is ignorant, students of man's diminution
and his honor whittled against the stature of magic and monkeys.

Caught in convergence, gay go

                              (the green lawns shall sear, the
      gracious
and not exceptional houses roar in collapse of drowning
brick; sky glare with gas, and vultures over the playground).

Our world, your world, little world, green go, go gay.

      As time drips
      the doll's head
      jerks.

            Then
      silence hoods,
      gathers, grows
      big.

         Abrupt on black
      crinklecrash thundersplits
      forlorn smoking halves.

Nobody even picked up the pieces. Pitiful
and forgotten the splintered city, fluttersmoke
wisping, scattered the track of footbeats vanishing.
They would not tidy their garbage. But no matter.
As reeking midden mounded to buttersoft landscape
and slept, and forgot history, the northmen bent
west from their casual wreckage. Children these
were; meant no harm and had no manners.
They circled back on the strong places, smashed
and rebuilt the beetling citadels; married

      / 86 /

their slaves; gracious grew, with just kings
and large liberal populations. The work
of their hands stops our breath. Their speech
strong flex, sweet wisdom, world's wonder.

> They, not we. Piled under
> drift of time, white harbor
> is sand reach by glitterblue of lonely sea.

> The friends were busy elsewhere.
> There were not enough swords.
> The potential was not there.
> Someone wasted the hoards
> of gold, or lost them. They fought,
> but they could never have won.
> The guards were asleep, or bought.
> They were done.

Sleep, city.
Let the murderous magnificence pass in Nineveh
howling above your grave; in Egypt hugely serious
over her meaningless mysteries of superstition, serene
contemplation of her narcissus in sacred waters.
Strip stark the splendors, male and female, of Sparta; webswathe
the sheathed and subtle, violet Athens:
Greece, the heartless and haunting in broken glitter of bluesleeved
    islands.

Sombre Rome outreaches, cramps
you in iron of difficult sinew. Ossifies,
turns rotten in the softer parts.

Saracen bigot and mailed murderous monk
squabble across your grave.

Perhaps you were worth the lot of them: for whom,
at least, a marriage is worth as much as a death:
who love men more than Man:
who would rather have the uninteresting town square rustle on
   Saturday night than have their name written on another part
   of the map.

The whole boiling, rank, incestuous kettle of history throws up
   here and there a radiant splash, which shines and is gone.

Undreamstirred sleep, which is little enough, is left you.
Sleep on, my city.
Sleep.

5

The Autumn Cleaning

I tear the past, the lives, the paper brains,
the scripts of scenes, the faces, in a pile
of soiled business, letters too late to answer,
obsolete obligations privately
commingled with an imperfect romance
here, there a blotted grudge, the universe
of paper.

        Photos. Here's a face. The eyes biggen.
Out.

    But two faces more, changed so, so keep.
Be sentimental.

        Old class lists, who were
these people, yes, but I remember *you.*
The University of Illinois
PhD 1935. Keep that.
This says one hundred fifty-six a month
upon retirement at age 65.
For the steel file. The paper world performs
futures as well as memories.

        Top drawer.
A pipe. A rubber band. A Chinese stamp.
At Pei-tai-ho the decorous donkeys' ears
and bells and trot emerged at Lotus Hills
on the right, and Tiger Rocks, and Black Leg Bay,
rolled in my drumming ear the shell's thunder
caught from last summer's surf, unsealed in blue.

Now read typed stanzas (if I can!) composed
of headlines and the Battle of Britain. *No,
but it was made of boredom and the blanks
of duty time and nothing to do, the cross-
word puzzle solved or stuck, staring at the blue
trousers of the watch officer asleep
on the blond-oak table. Tarry a moment, there
is something else: the editorial gloss.
Praiseworthy technical accomplishment
but find no true emotion dum de dum.*
File in the burnbag. Tear the paper brains.

More photographs. How mountains flatten out.
*The crash and laughter of a great green wind
down Adirondack slopes. And she. And I.
The cold pool by the rock, the ferns, and heaven.*

Maple by slant-crossed mullion and they wait
for me. I live. We'll to the woods again.
*The young green heron squatting in his swamp
snapped at the water, wrinkled mercury, spattered
the cathedral hush in a small wet noise.*

I tore my past. Brains and blood into ink
is painful transmutation, but when leaves
are torn so, there is pity in it. What lives
in the waste basket now, I shall not know.

Captive

After Theognis

I gave you wings. Black stone, blue heave shall take
the shadow of your flight. Where men pass, where
legend is live with music, they will make
your name a song, and you will still be there
when all your bones are gathered underground
to sad and private darkness in the sty
of Hades; you shall live still in the sound
of singing. Even dead you shall not die.
For song is mine and I am yours. Then go.
Continents dip behind your heel, appears
Ocean and spinning water miles below.
You ride on wind and a defeat of years.
I made you this. And now you turn from me
as from a child who will not let you be.

In the Beginning

There was a first time without anything to remember.
There was a nerve strung in wet shining southward
and the wheels striding over and over
the piston doubled and falling, and the sound
over thinking, and the rails' gleam;
the secret towns, their balance of despair
on caped hills, their tenses of color changing,
Cora, Lanuvium lost to the left, and seaward
the slow green heave of the campagna, screens
about a headlong nothing, a not-yet
folding into an alien dimension
as limestone folds to landscape sealed with blue
of scarfed water and history.

All that time waiting.

But the way back was otherwise, framed
in Campanian yesterdays, and always backward
piled on each other (with your fingers holding
time is lost in the drift). There is another reason
not to throw our nets into the black water
to drag what thin silver of reminiscence.
But if you and I ever need to remember:
our island plunged in rain, and was not there.
The promontories cut cool water level
to yellow bases; the water lifting backward
bared the coast a slant of gray to the drift,
and seaward to the mist Misenum

a fist of peril, and Cumae ever seaward
lit by no mortal sunset. Backward ever
we had the breathing mountain, the earth's anger
buckled under our knees; on the black, sidewise,
crescents of electricity; we had
a mile of sand at Paestum, even before it
a bridge at night between trees . . .

                    If you ever
need to remember, there is one more image
dropped on the shining heap: the mailed knights
asleep in effigy, the vandal sword, the drift
of surprised death, the skeletons of cities,
the strangers with eyes full of sunset and water
unmeasured homeward. There is another leaf
to make once more numberless the leaves
drifted to earth in thirty hundred Octobers,
if we ever need to remember . . .

                 But this is another
time before memory (come, your fingers
on my wrist, myself larger by one person
now, for the way beyond words of your being near me).
We could throw all this away, as we put aside
that island the death of a soul might once have bought
for a moment. We shall not ever need
to remember, any more, there is too much elsewhere.

Past Equinox and Up

Time, now and forever, climb the year and wheel
the hot stars up: burn sun, sluice rain, burst plant, explode
our thunderblush of April and unreel
the winter sleep of animals: hop, crawl toad
and snake wriggle: poison plant close fondle fresh
blooms. Now is the indiscriminate resurrection of the flesh
and shatterfall and pinflash of pain on eyeball and finger-
     ball that feel.

Take it, oh hold it close and close. Outgrows
bigger than ever your brain bulged it in dreams the shape
of the year. This dripping flail of thorns shall end in a rose
to end your roses all, her sprays escape
imagination, all that in cold sleep and the blind
of the year blossomed inside the garden shell of the mind
take, clasp till it cuts and sticks in the wound, tighten and
     hold it close:

and now: before the brute To-Be, the slow
ox with a fist clumps down the hill and clubs our bones
to dust. Splash once first, struggle. Not for our sweets, no.
Bare shivers the philosopher's anticipation when his stones
are slabs on what has been our fiction. No, but to see
the bruise blacken and wear our personal mark where we
hold, twist, grapple the year before the year goes
     where we also go.

Return of the Image

What symbol resurrects your spring?

For you were not ever seemingly even in our
intangible past habitation. No echoes ring
your voice. There is not any power

to charm that silhouette of flesh and essence
into more than the contour of ideals.
What symbol resurrects your presence
against a curtain in the mind that feels

only an absence not too large for regret?
It is because of your right and form, too strict
in style of grace ever like ours to be let
drift, a material derelict

populated by ghosts, about those mortal springs
where once your apparition stood
gathered about by afternoon as with wings
of future folding in the maytime wood,

or in the room, with the sun through the glass
dropping light from your wrist against the wall.
Are these things idols behind you? Do they pass
shining behind your life? Does any symbol recall

your transition through another person's shadow
with open eyes and with unfaltering feet?

Will you return, a stranger, to our living meadow
in voice and color complete?

And shall I see your outline on the wall?
Does any symbol recall?

Prothalamium

Before we remember this
not yet to be remembered
time, in the time that is,
take these periods ambered

in uncertainty, know
these minutes: edge on bright,
birch on green, gold on snow;
turn your hair in the light,

wrist in water, recall
the not yet, sun in your sleeves
gathered; young winds that fall
to the throat; the lying in leaves;

sand between waves, and between
rocks color, and cold blue
skyward in shallows green
your legs, sun drowning through.

Wind on your throat, recall
the not yet capture and flight
where the shining moments fall
the other side of tonight.

Midsummer Night

(Uncle Matthew, why can you not be wholly serious?)

Silvered in the slow loops of streams and caught
in compass of tamed bliss by countryside
where north goes pale and kind in night and June
to bend gray over green of meadows and wash
the clubbed spinneys to islands on its pallors,
the gothic city pondered (arched and groined
as groves of stone and mediaeval thought,
or Christopher and Queen Anne with domes and courts
bestride the silence of stilled traffic) on her past
told over and over in the bells of her names
(Saint Mary and Saint Peter-in-the-East,
Magdalen, tower and deer park, Oriel
of the Window, Corpus Christi and Tom Quad,
Merton of Duns, and Queens, and Folly Bridge).
Bemused by time's suspension in an orb
calmed by Thule's cream and Hyperborean gray,
the stone-enchanted metaphysician watched
ontology's escape in mullion panes
and moon, and latinists lost Latin. Out
beyond the lights and streets in distant pubs
sounds lapsed, and drinkers dreamed across their beers.

The year at point of turning seemed to hang.

The last train hooted, the last bus wheeled home.

Time gentlemen please.

/ 100 /

The watchman of the dome
clanged out one hundred one.

            In Long Meadow,
by Witham or on Headington Hill, at Bagley
Wood or dark on Shotover, the clerk
hand in hand with his starveling beauty, the lonesome
undergraduate, the don's daughter,
the strayed tourist and the strayed tourist's wife
caught the reverberations of the hour
and knew love's loss and the glum stride of time.

Two Octobers

Circle of gold on gold the year is kind
enough to bind
October on October and the ghost
of a touch lost
between emerges. Take my hand and shut
your eyes; your foot
is deep between Orion and our prime,
your foot prints time,
and the gold month rolls slowly back to green
shining between
slatewater of Nemi and the golden bough,
then and now
forever handfast, and I thought we went
over the bent
hills to Frascati and the pale sweet wine
yours and mine
forever as the forest in between
gold into green
is changed and changed. In yesterday's strong lines
tomorrow shines
unwritten but remembered and lived through.
I thought you knew
how this collapse of spinning color fills
the Alban hills
forever and not-yet, and that it means
all in-betweens
and all our year has gathered up its sleeves
across the leaves.

/ 102 /

Legend for a Shield

Legend married April and death to breed this
branch of green strength. Trees understand, the rain is
bright accomplice, only our eyes are vexed with
     sun, nor perceive it.

Half your destiny is as gold and amber
luminous. Wear this, and reject that iron
frail with use crossbound to your blazon. Be with
     leopard and gryphon

clear and fierce in mystery, when the skilled lips
bend across your eyes, and you watch the arms' grace
turn and fold, be history, and the charmed eyes
     model your future.

Strike then, innocent and savage, be ware of
April in your star. For a man before you
took the devious way, and his blood remembers
     here, in this poem.

Autumn Equinox

Shoulders in the thin angle of elm the boy watches
his month burn out in maple and sumach, wish drowning
in steep sunfall bannered under the cold skyline.

Reluctant the red lingers, sky-flush west. Red is
the kiss he took to bed last night; the tide beating
wrist to close heart; an answer; a silk dress captured.

This was farewell and love-no-longer. White hesper
and tamarack scratch now punctuate the steel progress
of night's tomorrow climbing up the cold autumn.

Five o'Clock

These afternoons of nerve and tissue raise
islands evocative of elsewhere, lost
in the torn gauze of unhistoric days;
lands raw with sunlight, which the retinal ghost

remembers, never having seen; the snow
in feathered mist; the gryphon on the gold;
the slain who walk; the tall black king whose bow
no northern arm could bend. Oh, it was told

myself, and by myself, how on a time
the color of an angel's hair was strung
across my heart. Untrue, untrue. The rhyme
broke out its future when the hand was wrong

who now ropes back his drifted swans to lie
docile as boats in place upon the film
of evening colored water, and not fly
the arrogant sunlight of that young, false realm

where snow and gold and death compact by art
are penance to chastise the winter heart.

Anniversary

Where were we in that afternoon? And where
is the high room now, the bed on which you laid your hair,
as bells beat early in the still air?

A two o'clock of sun and shutters. Oh, recall
the chair's angle a stripe of shadow on the wall,
the hours we gathered in our hands, and then let fall.

Wrist on wrist we relive memory, shell of moon
on day-sky, two o'clock in lazy June,
and twenty years gone in an afternoon.

The Shadowgraphs

Image comes down to live as fact, and turns
in the same motion, and is memory. The process
climbs my long gallery, jogs the score, and burns
in points of color, fancy, and, ah yes,
love. For the same finesse
that changed my copper counters into gold
falters not, sleeps not ever, nor grows old.

What then have I not done, what have I done
with *sometimes*, *not*, and *never*, how to list
my loss against my gain when all are one
and on the vision's glad and deceived mist
the blonde illusionist
performs before my captured audience
her same and golden chores of innocence?

Here is a march of fictions down the road
to nowhere and forever. Did I live
these dolls of faith or die that episode
of fury? Who knows now? Pale, through a sieve
drained days combine to give
substance of what? Who knows? Never goodbye
while the deft hand is sweeter than the eye.

It

(For S.L. and A.L., who think of writing)

Do it, then. If you do,
incontrovertibly know
the worst thing you have done
is the best thing under the sun
if it was written true,
if it was meant to be so.

Never write to please.

A poem is a not-yet.
Then, as you make it, forget
what you imagine to be
the critic who can't read,
the reader who can't see.

Make it alone for you
and yourself.
         Choose
what you mean to do.
But it will be no use.
It will choose you.

You took no life of ease.

Think of the world when you
are in the world. If it will

/ 108 /

the world will judge. When you write,
a blind maker, alone
in your individual night,
be steel, be stone.
The world may tear it from you
in its day, when you are through.
If not, you have made it still.

Despise temperament.
Beyond all else despise
the trick of lineament,
the look of the hair and eyes,
the professional veneer,
the Needs of your Career.
Poets as such are dull.
The poem is all.

Live only to understand
only the thing in your hand,
the sight that sticks in your eye,
the wish that sticks in your heart
and will not let you be
until it is made art.